woman
unfolding

woman
unfolding

by Jenna Mervis

modjaji books

Publication © Modjaji Books 2011
Text © Jenna Mervis 2011

First published in 2011 by Modjaji Books Pty Ltd
P O Box 385, Athlone, 7760, South Africa
modjaji.books@gmail.com
http://modjaji.book.co.za
www.modjajibooks.co.za

ISBN 978-1-920397-33-3

Book and cover design by Natascha Mostert

Printed and bound by Mega Digital, Cape Town
Set in Palatino

Earlier versions of these poems have appeared
in *New Contrast*, *New Coin* and *Carapace*.

For mom and dad,
with love.

Acknowledgements

I am grateful to all the people who
have helped me on my poetic journey.
To Geoffrey Haresnape for his keen
supervision over the course of my
Masters Degree in Creative Writing,
during which some of these poems
were written. And to Beverley Rycroft
for her meticulous editing eye. I am
forever grateful to Colleen Higgs for
taking me under her Modjaji wing and
publishing this collection.

Thanks to my family for giving me
the space to write, and for their
unconditional support. A special
thanks to my mom /chief-editor /
unrelenting-wordsmith /fiercely-loyal-
fan, without whom I wouldn't be where
I am today.

Finally to Justin, who courageously
married a poet, despite the inherent
risks. Thank you.

Contents

Jump In!

Jump in! I'm shivering pot-bellied
silicone-capped for a cold water
swim, there's drizzle, the water's dark
blue and I can see the crocodile
mosaiced at the bottom of the pool:
he has swallowed a child before me.

Dive in! Now I'm slick black-strapped
costume queen with long arm strokes
and foamy kicks that keep me stationary;
red-crowned buoy girl off the mark
with an aquatic slap, a snort to sink
then launch off the crocodile's head: up for air.

Move in! We're skinny-dipper racers
on your marks, doubled over, block
mounted, gun-ready to plunge in.
My crocodile has paddled to another
pond where new children tickle his scales.
So, hold my hand, show me how deep to dive.

Before Each Woman

Be careful!

Our mother left the mantra
at the front door,
an Elijah cup
of worry,
then whizzed off
in the stationwagon.

It felt like oneword,
a blessing –
sipping from the Kiddush cup
on a Friday night –
like some kind
of Sabbath savvy.
Just one taste,

then pass it on.
We galloped
across the lawn –
stampeding wild horses –
her *becareful's* ensconced
like snails on a hot day.
We grew tired, forgetful.

Before each woman
there is a girl
skipping in the margins
like unpractised cursive
dipping in
and out of the rules.
Which is why

it was no surprise
that, later,
ravenous and grubby,
fingers stretching
for the biscuit tin,
I swallowed a ten cent coin.
Without choking.

An accidental ingestion
lacking consequence.
No medical drama.
Just a lesson that what goes in
must, eventually, come out,
polished but
unchanged.

Poems Are Daughters Too

You say it so politely
gently turn the page:
please take off your clothes

I accompany my poem on her first visit
into the consultation room, hold her hand
while you feel for lumps in her text.
You count her ova as syllables –
find the rhythm disturbed and irregular
in the polycystic verse.
I hate that you know her secrets.

I want to comfort my poem,
say *everything's going to be okay.*
You ease cold hard reason
into her body,
scrape words off her lines
test them for weakness,
analyse the meaning.
She turns to me, on her back,
legs bent and spread,
and stares into my eyes .

I hold her hand while you finish.
Help her reshape, re-cover
while you look away.

I sit dumb through the interrogation:
Are you regular (no)
Is your flow heavy (yes, when it comes)
Is there pain (there's always pain)
I watch you scrawl a prescription.

For some reason,
I feel violated,
for some reason
I feel responsible.

Inflation

Remember that old one rand coin
with the springbok fixed mid-leap
over the nickel veld?
That shiny silver disc
transformed every child's world
into liquorice and chappies and wicks
and granadilla blimps
hovering over sticky fists.

Little girls and boys consumed
banks of the stuff
over a school year.
We got given one each –
a treat saved for civvies day
when we could throttle each other
on the playground
or jump rope or roll marbles or spit
out of uniform.

In a tuck shop queue
one rand meant
chips, a chocolate milk
and a startling fizzer
that could wrap its pink tentacles around molars
suction loose teeth from the gum –
small pleasures
absent in home-packed lunch.
There in the palms of our hands
our coins would nest
like golden eggs
full of promise.

Remember those slightly ridged edges
like a Free State escarpment?
The heads on the back,
the coat of arms for tails?
They could buy milk and bread.
Then only milk.
Then only bread.
Then just chappies.
Then not even the gum.
The springbok's frozen leap,
becoming smaller, lighter
as we grew
bigger
heavier
up.

School Outing

Two by two
rhyming couplets
perfectly small and trim
they hold hands loosely
not knowing loss.
Some forget, some skip
out of line
out of teacher time.
Tap dancing
into the museum
they meet
T-rex, Neanderthal Man, Coelacanth,
Another School,
then lunch amongst stuffed
wildlife
fishpaste sandwiches
taxidermy.
They meet a mummy,
make jokes
while pushing back against
a friend, shifting away,
herding each other from death.
They meet
the curator
watch his corners foam
watch the bubbles pop
off his chin
as he pours
past tense
into perfectly hemmed laps –
empty vessels
too full of the present
to hear.

Games

Hop-scotch skipping rope marbles
marco polo blind man's bluff charades.
In the games we play with each other
together or against there is one winner.

Only one of us can lose the games you play
with each other (with me) guess wrong
miss a beat or a count if you cannot find
me (I am hiding) you cannot see me

(I am hiding) in your games you play
with us, mostly with me, there is no love
only five four three two one war of wit
no love, simply a girl and a boy hiding.

Good Boy

(for Oscar)

We climb quietly
into the night,
padding the hot grey tar.
You move sideways
with difficulty,
pulling towards grass
and familiar gates
your cricket click nails
syncopating the effort.
Dogs fall like dominoes
into barking and braying
at our scent intrusion.
I pause to breathe,
sponge the moist air
taste the sea
rolling on my tongue.
Remember how we ran
as waves transformed the dunes
with plankton light?
Now we shuffle together
a poet and her dog –
a parched story-teller
and a veteran
of over-breeding.
You stop at every tree
as if it were your last.
Urine still comes
when bidden,
now slides down your legs
onto your paws.

At home I kneel down
wash each foot and leg.
You lean into my shoulder
heavy, exhausted, curious.
I stroke your mane
follow its thinning
down your spine
to that scabbed skin.

Beneath my hand
your back legs collapse
a folded marionette
sorry boy.
You straighten awkwardly,
I watch your body twist
muscles shiver.
good boy.

Later, alone,
you climb quietly
into the night ,
hands holding your face
your paws
your great sagging body.

Starting Over

what if love
dries out your mouth

like too much red wine
or talking through the night?

what if love leaves
your tongue

swollen, stuck
against your palate

and your lips
cracked closed

unable to speak
without tearing?

Promises

He said once *I want to be*
with you for the rest of my life.

I am left alone with the bleak day
defending its promise like a cub
a bloody carcass, wanting play
more than meat, needing reaction,
some kind of response. The flay
of flesh reminds me I love deeply,
not often, but thoroughly.

He may graft to me, bud to stem,
fuse his scion vows to my stock
love me doggedly or bodily
or sturdily and still not stay.

The Thought Of You

I've had your image framed
I've captured you –
pressed you between
glass palms
in prayer.
I've contained you.
I can take you with me
when I go.
If you go.

You are standing
watching me leave.

I am leaving
with your framed face.
Not love, not yet.
Just the thought of you.

Exodus

For mom.

A shadowless,
careless day,
fruit pickers
bumble-beeing in trees,
the sawmills
churning wood,
sugar fields
burning since dawn.

An ordinary day
like any other
an unnoticed leaving
but for your body
hipping the door
wedged ship
run aground.

I cling to my raft
drifting further
away from you.

Looking Back

State Highway 75, Arthur's Pass, New Zealand.

Long road:
haiku me
after this goodbye.

Asphalt surges
east to west
channelled by
scree slopes and snow.

I stand sentinel
at one end
with hoisted flag

(I have arrived,

I am leaving)

I watch her

drive away,

a mouthful of pitch
to caulk the void.

Silent World

When you begin to plumb,
the mind is an unfathomed ocean.

I've charted mine on my palm –
only the knowable parts, my fist
clamped like a clam on low tide –
it is safer this way.

My aunt visits a therapist. Together
they plunge off an even keel
like two Jacques Cousteaus
plummeting down
sinking
buddy breath
by breath
into her silent world.

There are no whales down there.
No silver bubble streams
or gasps of big blue
no steadfast turtles
no mantas to swift her to surface.

There in the ridges and trenches
of that unfathomable sea
hand in hand
they trawl
for something:

a coelacanth
a wreck

a scream
to echolocate.

Another Shore

I am a substitute. My life has flowed
Into another channel
And I do not recognise my shores.
                    from Anna Akhmatova 'Northern Elegies'

This body
is without mind
which is
elsewhere, harboured
dry docked,
tipping
effentjies
to the side
as if the vessel
holds
memory of
gently slanting
swells
or diagonal gulls
diving
on a fine day.

This body, without
mind,
is two feet two legs
beached, flailing
one vagina one stomach
a solitary churning
below
two propeller breasts,
arms,
hands.
One drawbridge mouth
dropped shut.
The rest –
nose, eyes, ears –
barnacles suctioned
to skin.

This body-without-mind,
does not recognise
its shore
because it is
without
mind
And I do not recognise my shores.

On A Train To St Andrews, Scotland

I was born
in the caul of your veld,
encased in your accent.
Because of you
I am migratory,
your geography
tattooed on my skin
in sun spots,
these tan lines
washed up
on my breasts.

I've been gone too long.
I step so lightly
in this new life
no trace of living
or leaving:
a bird on the wing.

Where are swallows
when they are home?

Settling

I
I climb a hill one dry Eastern Cape day, to see where our settlers
went.
At the summit, a monument with engraved compass
charts the settlers' routes, records passages of ships and people:
lines of ants, touching feelers and moving on.
I see nothing but veld, and in the distance, an informal settlement.

II
se'ttle[2] *v.* **1.** *v.t.* & *i.* ~ **(down)**, to establish or become established
in more or less permanent abode or place or way of life

Moving with armfuls of roots clutched to our breasts,
a tangled mass of entrails not our own, we are unearthed.

III
settle ~ (down) (cause to) cease from wandering or motion or
change or disturbance or turbidity (*things will soon settle into
shape; marry and settle down; settle down to married life;*)

Where is the map to mark the man-made marriages of our
past – our women shipped to foreign shores and stripped
on make-shift bridal beds, settled into silence,
muddy fingered children taking root at their feet?

IV
Mordant, schizophrenic settle. We must plant ourselves
yet you cannot settle yourself on one stem, obese rhizome!
Sending up multiple meanings, conflicting demands,
undermining us.

V
Yet we will settle. We
are finding space, planting ourselves,
waiting for the roots to take.

Cul-de-Sac

One learns the signs:
the cynical smiles,
the red feathered sclera
of sleepless nights.
Friends come and go
like dandelion whiskers
on a kittenish breeze.
Never settled
never domesticated
except when sleeping or fucking.
The body is their only home.

They leave in search of whiteness –
elsewhere – like some bleached Shangri-La,
or shoulder their homes
in search of some other world's otherness.
The nostalgic friends
the when-we's
the if-we's, the if-only's
don't know why they left
or can't remember.
Conversations spin towards
that single point of return,
then topple over.
Behind the backs of their barbeques
they whisper: *braai!*

These migratory men and women
walk the well-worn circuit of dislocation
that doldrum cul-de-sac
where a dog chases its tail,
a garden sprinkler spins water
clicking into each rotation,
where a child
pedal-creaks a tricycle,
round and round
and round.

Shedding Skin

Standing over your grave now
granddaughter is brittle,
splitting down my spine.
Cracks vein across my shoulders,
fissures gape.
I push through,
cast off the worn skin.

There are degrees of loss.
Mostly the loss of oneself in another:
myself in you.
The loss of appellation.
Moulting relationships,
an epithelial loss.
I catch myself
grasping
for the next skin.

My translucent old self,
imprinted with granddaughter,
rises and falls
as your last breath.

I walk away pink and raw.

Navigation

Your body is my country.
In the familiar borders of your provinces
navigating roads across your contours
I know I am home.

Your shoulders are the Karoo.
Fine fynbos hairs break the surface
against my cheek, I inhale
dust and dry riverbeds.
Your ground is covered in spoor.
A lonely korhaan *stokstil,*
clicks and shrills,
splitting your stillness.

Your back is the Breede River.
I finger each vertebra
searching for your source.

I survey your horizon.
Two roads stretch out
spun with veins to guide me,
scars to signpost the way.

South, below your stomach,
so many paths
thick and forested.
I track your caves, your mountains
lose myself in the peaks,
Marble Baths of your skin.

Your skin is a night sky
I follow the stars to your face.

The Quiet House

In the quiet house
a daily hush hangs
like mist in a valley
drifts past furniture
through floorboards
beneath closed doors,
in the quiet house.

Outside the quiet house
the muted morning mouths
a truck leaning
on brakes downhill,
a pneumatic drill
coughing up
bone-dry dust,
a barking dog,
the creepy crawly's shudder,
gutturals of pavement patter,
outside the quiet house.

In the quiet house,
a poet mimes melodies
with commas and stops
a punctuated silence
hyphened, speechless,
each mouse-click
on castanet keyboard
a cacophony of creation
in the quiet house,
where sound is shut out.

Salad

Caught in the heart
of a lettuce
a pocket of air
with a garden
in full spring
warm as a compost heap.

Held to the ear:
a galaxy of germinating seeds
swelling, colliding,
Vivaldi
or Holst's The Planets,
activity like star bursts
and solar flares.

There is little else
to the salad:
tomato, cucumber, carrot, rocket,
a dressing as usual –
though the heart
needs no
camouflage.

Harvest

My sister returns
from her garden
with a basket
of granadillas,
sun-baked
and intoxicating.
I take one
without asking
pierce the warm skin,
tear a hole for my lips
then suck and slurp
the sticky seeded syrup
of summer harvest
giddy in the shade.

February Disa

I stand at the foot
of a waterfall carpeted in moss.
Dense mats filter water
in persistent trickles
despite this dry summer.
Polished shelves jut out
stacked like a Tetris game –
angular, irresistibly soft.
I press my hands
into the sponge
lift up my face
into falling diamonds.
Sun skids to the canopy edge
catapults over,
and there: skewered
in a soft green cloud
way above me
this three-petalled
kamikaze pilot
blazing red.

The Tourist

He comes to Cape Town
to paint a house:
inside, outside, undercoat, final coat.
He is brought from Durban
for three weeks
to paint.

The first Saturday he's given a tour.
The car snakes along the coast
and over the neck of a mountain,
he is told, people climb at full moon.
At the harbour they point across to Robben Island.
He squints into the distance,
So is that where the Old Man lived?
The ships are Signal Reds,
Mauritian Blues, Matterhorn Whites;
applications of coat on salty coat.
He runs a hand along the hull
I know boats.

The second Saturday he walks to the beach,
wades into icy water
warming at the river mouth.
Kelp nooses his ankles,
tightening, pulling on the ebb.
He backs out, looks upriver
to thickets of reeds.
Are there crocodiles?
Sand stuccos his wet feet.
I know crocodiles.

On the last Saturday,
sitting on the top rung
he squeezes bristles
between thumb and forefinger;
slips the paintbrush into his back pocket.
He has done what he came to do
(inside, outside, undercoat and final coat).
Tomorrow I rest.
He climbs down.
I know tomorrow.

The Waiting Room

My daily clock-in at the screen
begins with a mouthful of cereal
to the hum of a fan on a hot day.
From above, I watched you leave,
spied your curled crown between
the wisteria's tendrils and lilac sprays,
kept you in sight until the fourth step.
I know well what comes after –
a key turning, then the splutter of a tired
engine you keep meaning to service
then the scrape of rubber on tar
then an absence of noise, a breach
in daily sounds of builders and dogs
as we all stop to watch you go.

There are things to be done,
'woman' things like laundry and dishes –
tasks you always saved for weekends.
And this brain of mine is in limbo,
waiting for some kind of response
so that I can move forward
get on with other things, other projects.
I am a car in neutral, idling.

I'm envious of the purpose to your waking –
the way you peel out of bed confident, naked.
You know where you are going: to work,
to that desk claimed as your territory
with photographs of me.
And you know what you must do,
until you return home, definite as a full-stop,
to me. I am a plastic carry bag, snagged, stuck.

Is this how it feels to be lost? Pushing against
the world, contracting into oneself, nauseous?
To gradually sink beneath communication
reverting to cavernous grunts and sighs,
typing, not talking. Mute. I am, I am
a compass needle. I am static, out of range.

And when you return home to me, I find
a purpose enclosed in your arms, in the shoes
you kick off, in your unbuttoned shirt.
Then you ask what I've been doing
and I pack away the truth behind white lies
and fold in fables of a full day
because I have left most of myself
upstairs in my room of waiting.

Unfolding

After reading 'Portrait of Love' by Njabulo S. Ndebeble

There is my husband-to-be,
my fiancé, bent
over the garden tap
with deliberate hands
barefoot, sweating in
the midday glare
with shadow dog beside him
that thrusts a wet nose
into his neck. There!
See that almost-husband of mine
and his capable fingers
his calculating mind
and Wednesday's re-growth
coarse against my skin
this morning before coffee
when he took my hand
passed it over his face
to kiss my palm
and murmur his desire.

There! There he is, my betrothed.
I watch from the window seat,
piled with crumpled linen
ready to be folded
and shelved
and see our life
beyond this frame,
unfold the rolling years
to that familiar point
where this pubescent union
of ours is forgotten,
this merging of two children,
led by the nose into adulthood.

There he is,
my darling promised,
becoming man
as I become woman,
unfolding into him.

Pearl

For Justin, 15th March 2009

A disappointing oyster
pried open
gapes,
and another
and another,
empty.

Your smile
does things to me
I shouldn't write here
and when I part
your lips
my tongue
touches bliss.

And we'll marry
on the ides of march
because it is our day
as any other,
and we'll want
for nothing.
We'll peel the flesh
from its marbled shell
and find,
yes!
our pearl.

Birthday

This day separates at dawn.
Its lachrymal whey crusts my eyes,
curds thick as clouds
on my tongue.
I feel heavier, headier,
another year older.

This tally
of determined hooves
on track towards the finish,
measures my waning
in fractions of length.

Why do I celebrate this start
if I can't remember the snap
of race gates,
the sting of a whip
or the roaring crowd?

And why do you celebrate
my tote of life lived and not yet lived
re-run year after dogged year?

Then I see you both
in your front row seats,
keen spectators,
eyes fixed on my course.

And I realise that all this time
it's your colours
I've been wearing.

Winter From A Balcony

five o clock winter sun on the mountainside breaks
through clouds in zigzag shine between icicle
gums; there's more rain in those grey tenements
overhead, more chilled rasps of air to be inhaled
or fought off with fleece and fake fur; even the eyes
are cold enough to freeze tears, and snot stops short
of nostrils' thresholds crusting like stalactites and mites;
I'm pissing coffee, tea, hot anything from the kettle;
clasped tight to my stomach is a bottle of warmth
and later a man who'll turn in at night with his hot
head and warm-blooded panting to heat our sheets;
or an electric blanket you can't marry or cook for
but want to kiss each time you crawl under its skin;
time drags the sun across the sky like a reluctant dog
bucking at the end of its leash not another step further
on its nimbostratospheric chain soaked with rain –
the cumulative effect of afternoons like this one; even
the house shivers and curses, brick by brick, the drizzle.

Dog-day Afternoon

if I get any closer to the heater I'll catch alight no doubt like my poor
dog who is pacing the house in wide circles an eternally combusting
engine never quitting until he is sent to bed to watch the rain through
the glass door

but it's pouring I tell him nicely first then roughly because his
whimpering is beginning to give me a headache but you can't reason
with a forty kilogram metabolic mutant that would fetch tennis balls
in monsoon season Sumatra if he could

each week his trainer insinuates he is spoiled when he doesn't sit
when asked or told and it makes me wonder why we bothered
sparing the rod at his weekly lessons but its not her fault I let him curl
into bed with me so I can fall asleep to his heartbeat

nor that I don't really care if he doesn't come when called because
even I'd rather chase mongooses than return for a biscuit or that being
jumped on wound around and licked is a cure-all for a long hard day
away from home

and I know what everyone's thinking: lets hope she's better with the
two legged kind well let's hope children don't whine on rainy days to
be let out of the house because by then this dog will have driven this
poet to the rod.

Birth Marks

My head is in your hands.
Water washes over my scalp
free-wheels down my temples
dripping blood-warm into my ears.
It is an exquisite submersion
this almost-drowning.

You gather my hair,
squeeze it dry,
staunch the water pooled
in the trough of each ear.
Then your hands!
Your strong hands
begin to move over my scalp
in a tidal purr
their touch drugging me,
drawing me downwards,
like gravity,
into an unsounded well.

I give to you
the weight of my head
let you hold it mid-air,
floating my thoughts
in your wet palms.
You cup my neck,
fingers flutter the follicles
at its base –

and then you stop.
I feel your thumb
brush that place
that is mine in reflection only –
that pink stain
marking my birth.

This shadow touch
this gentle shock of scarring
births our intimate instant
before you recoil,
allow my hair to fall back
as a veil.

You return to washing
and rinsing
and drying –
what you have witnessed
a curiosity
a tiny horror

pressed into your skin.

Posture

My physio calls the shape of my back a Cell C curve
and I can see for myself
slouched in front of the mirror
that she is not wrong.
push your pelvis down
Which I do – when I find it that is –
until my spine unfurls into an s-shape
and I feel oddly upright
drop your ribs
lengthen your neck, C2 to C6
Which I try, I swear I do,
but I can't locate the muscles to lower the ribs
and my turkey neck is straining to isolate C2
in its vertebral alphabet
in order to elongate
and I feel like a National Geographic illustration
plotting early man's evolution
into homo erectus.

This is my body in stretch and flex:
a bent wire.

If muscles have memory,
then what if they never forget
my failures and losses?
Each day another kink
in the wire mesh,
the creased skin at the base of my head
just a sheet slept on too many times.
Then it's not back ache I suffer,
but nostalgic interspinals
and regretful intercostals,
and a torso transformed into
a muscular scrapbook.

What if good posture depends
on a mind sitting upright
and all my efforts
are preposterous?

Wish

There is a thing I wish for,
a coda to my every day,
that I wish only for you.
A simple, singular hope
sunburnt and blistered
from over-exposure year
after year, wishbone after
wish bone, eyelash after
eyelash, shooting star
after shooting star.

It is a simple, singular hope,
this thing that I wish for you –
a passenger on the delicate hair
of a dandelion blown adrift.

And I continue to wish –
like a donkey turning a water wheel,
drawing from a coinless well.

An Extraordinary World

Each night I close my eyes in preparation,
stretch and tune each muscle
to my circadian clock's tick-tocking back beat.
My somnolent lullaby is nightjar flutes
and eagle owl bassoon hoots,
crickets strung and plucked,
and a porcupine's percussion shuffle.

I slow-breathe through this melody,
feel myself slipping into sleep...

I dream of steering from the back seat
with liquorice arms, losing control,

of fighting, throwing punch after jellied punch,
never making contact,

of flying over mountains with confident breaststrokes
dipping like a seal into a sea of grass...

until with hypnic
            skip
I trip back into night's gentle symphony
only to be lulled finally,
spindle-deep
into an extraordinary sleep.

Windfall

Today the beach is flattened out
the sea a giant roller
levelling and compressing
its run into shore.
I've brought my dog
for our daily leg-stretch-think
and to scour the shoreline
for driftwood and sea glass.

Zach fetch! And he's after the ball,
splattering water,
scattering schools of fry
that skim the shallows.
I call him back before he
reaches the lagoon:
a marshy sewer, shrunken,
stippled with white gulls
and mewling grey chicks
oblivious to the sign
shipwrecked in the sand
warning against bathing
or splashing barefoot.
In its fine print
people spit and shit
upstream because they
have nowhere else to go.

Zach come! And he's back
at my urgent side for an instant,
then off again, his long nose
on a honey bee dance
up the beach.
I follow his trail
wending through rotten kelp
and dead crabs
beached by yesterday's gales
to a man on his haunches
skinning two baby seals.
The blue-veined horror
of flesh freezes me.
He looks up, smiles,
these dead pups
a windfall
on a hot day.

An Illegal Trade

I've heard of a man
who skins poets
and sells their pelts
on the export market –
illegal trade, but lucrative.

A poet cannot live without skin.

There are people who
milk poets for their bile.
I've seen pictures of this:
a sedated body spread-eagled
on living room floor
bile pumping from
tube to jar
like thick black ink.

A poet cannot live without bile.

In Asia people slice off
the fingers of poets
as edible delicacies
once the reserve of the rich
now for a burgeoning
middle class;
in every ocean
hundreds of poets
float, fingerless, bleeding
on red currents.

A poet cannot live without fingers.

In Africa men take the whole hand.

A poet cannot live without hands.

And some men collect
those rare specimens of poet
who breathe through the skin,
or hatch only one poem in a lifetime.
They cage these poets,
suspend them from ceilings
like warm-blooded chandeliers
for guests to admire.

A poet cannot live without freedom.

You may not believe me,
but I've seen pictures of poets
without skin and without fingers,
and poets drained of bile, and poets
hornless, tuskless, eyeless. Poets
without hands, poets without venom;

And I'm telling you:
a poet cannot live without these things!

A world without poets
is as dark as bile
bled from black bears,
as toxic as venom
milked from captive snakes,
as fetid as rotting finless
carcasses of sharks
as disabled as a gorilla
without its hand.

You may not believe me,
but poetry is slipping
through our fingers
like fine sand

we will never
recover it.

Intrusion

I'm writing a poem
when Vatiswa calls me.
She holds a mat to her chest
like a shield, shrinks back to let me pass.
On wet cobblestones,
disturbed by her routine of shaking out carpets,
interrupted like the poem
on my roller top desk,
two furies recoil from us,
and the disorienting sunlight
sends them into flurries
of seething cursives
twisting together,
apart. Fits of arabesques.
A kind of poetic epilepsy.

I want them to stay at this threshold,
grant us our daily comings
and goings, sacred as our mezuzah,
so we can touch their brass cool skins
with our fingertips,
then to our lips in thanks
for their protection –
that they have chosen
this place above all others.

My poem is as I left it,
... *entwined,* it reads,
our sinuous bodies become ...
I've lost the intention,
forgotten where the words were going.

Perhaps we are not so different.
Snakes and lovers:
writhing ends with two bodies
splitting apart, searching for cover
beneath sheets or tall grass.
Seeking refuge from intrusion.

Elegy For Paul

(for Paul, d.12.06.2009 in Helmand province, Afghanistan)

In this cradle of hills
they still march
their Queen-beat
stiff-arm
rifle-flagging march
that hooked you,
pulled you
into poppy fields.

I see you now before me
would touch your face
this June day.
But you are gone
to ground.

A trumpet wails.
Remember Soho, Paul?
Remember
whiskey-tripping tongues
and drawn-out minors
marooning us at that table?
We jazzed and dreamed
of being poets
and novelists
and famous.

Shots slam the sky
seven soldiers salute
your new station
beneath our feet.

You've gone to ground
today Paul
to the sound of *Yitgaddal veyitqaddash*
we've laid you down.

I'm wearing black for you
today Paul,
its hue ironed
on my tongue.

Beached

Yesterday,
fifty five unfathomable ships washed ashore,
tidal helpers tugging and slipping,
watching whales die in weary waves
as a single bullet breached each bulkhead.

Today,
a flotilla of houses moored on a mountainside
dogs anchored to the shade
we spill over into wildness here at deck's edge
fynbos laps at our bare feet.

Tomorrow,
I see us beached in old age
your calcite skin, your sea glass eyes
you are coral, crumbling to sand
I am driftwood, bleached and bent.

We lie together on a percale shore
powerless to the inward press of time
I see a child, our grandchild, standing over us
small hands touching our slow death.

Not Yet

My nipples hurt
marking a premenstrual
rush of blood
to the head,
the flood of yet another
month, my ritual,
apothecarial relief.

An abandoned moon
tilts out of kilter above
the craggy silhouette
of this mountain setting.
One pill after the other
tracks her phases until
my body hardens
and ejects pre-life
like a pilot from a
doomed plane.

Whenever I get sick,
my mother asks:
Are you pregnant?
If only I could say yes,
extend my belly
push out my breasts
fall back into
her wishful arms.

Instead I meet her halfway:

at that point between generations,
in the succulent veld
of a young marriage.

Not yet, mom,
not yet.

Pipe-track

We take the car on the dirt this time.
First the sharp incline of loose wet
ground beneath our wheels
scrambling up to the level track
above main road
above smallholdings
and residential estates
above everything
except the Vlakkenberg's jagged peaks
that dwarf us regardless of how high we climb.

Below us, an exhausted coil of cars
snakes down towards the sea.
We crest the hill,
then follow the pitted wend of wet clay
carved into the mountainside
iced with fynbos and white stumps
like burnt out candles.

This place, in parts, is wrecked.
Aliens run rampant down slopes
somersaulting children
ripping up soil as they go –
and he says, my cynic husband,
survival of the fittest.

Yet there are Proteas in flower
and brazen sugarbirds
that flag down opponents
with long tail feathers
racing low to the ground
or spinning up towards the cliffs.

And there are eagles on the drift.
And fern-bedded gullies of water
and perennial streams
erupting onto the road.
Their obstinacy is infectious.

Stop I say, and I wind down my window.
What? he asks.
And I can smell it in the air –
I can even taste it:
this persistence of life
beyond control, or intrusion.

Nothing, it's nothing. Carry on.

Lists

1.
I awake to a roll call:
lists of lists
cataloguing do's and don'ts
meetings, dates, visits,
mailing lists
shopping lists
strata of actions and activities
stepped into a tedious ladder
its bottom rung as low
as the benthic bass of Johnny Cash;
a scale of duty ascending
to a mediocre middle tone.

2.
Oh! these lachrymose lists!

3.
On tangled sheets
my hands press into your chest
two clown fish
in thick anemone hair .
Your lips list my every inch
and I offer no resistance –
but for the run of your tongue
my parts would remain unchecked.

4.
glorious myopic moment –
only you in my sight
my taste
my touch!

5.
(Here on my back
on this unmade bed
on any given Sunday
I am flung to the
top-most rung.)

What Comes Next

(Remembering Giant's Causeway, Northern Ireland)

Milestones of our life
stretch out behind us
petrified markers of time,
our own Giant's Causeway
jutting from this vast sea,
eruptions of triumphs
and volcanic failures
stepping back
towards our birth shore.

We stand at it's rocky edge
facing our horizon.
What comes next
is for us to decide.
We wade deeper
into each other
like herons, hunting,
or cormorants
diving beneath water.
We feed on dreams.
We pursue our future,
swept on swift currents,
open-billed
gulping passion,
rising from the water
winged   missiles   up,
up! into our unknown.

What comes next
is for us to decide.
But look back –
turn your face
towards that causeway
of our past
and tell me,
I dare you to tell me
then,
that we will not last.

End Of Day

in a house bent
by violent gusts,
my desk lost
beneath notes
and bills, used
cups and saucers;
everything's at angles
even our dog's head
cocked, listening to
a pianist next door
climbing scales
in skewed minors;
even the two pigeons
sunning on our lawn,
wings fanned and lopsided
tipped by the wind.

another end of day
waiting for your return
surveying a sun-stained sky
turbulent as an ocean.
I drop
a plumb line
for happiness
stand like a
drunken clock,
just short of five.

Other poetry titles by Modjaji Books

Fourth Child
by Megan Hall

Life in Translation
by Azila Talit Reisenberger

Burnt Offering
by Joan Metelerkamp

Oleander
by Fiona Zerbst

Strange Fruit
by Helen Moffett

Please, Take Photographs
by Sindiwe Magona

removing
by Melissa Butler

Missing
by Beverly Rycroft

These are the Lies I told you
by Kerry Hammerton

The Suitable Girl
by Michelle McGrane

Conduit
by Sarah Frost

http://modjaji.book.co.za